JONATHAN DOVE

They will rise

for SATB Choir and Organ

EDITION PETERS

LEIPZIG · LONDON · NEW YORK

They Will Rise

But those who hope in the LORD will renew their strength;
They will rise, they will soar, they will fly up on wings like eagles;
They will run and not grow weary;
March on and not feel faint.

– Isaiah 40:31

Duration: 5′

Commissioned by the Dean and Chapter of Westminster and first performed at a service on 10th July 2018 to commemorate the centenary of the Royal Air Force by the Choir of Westminster Abbey with Peter Holder (organ), conducted by James O'Donnell

In memory of Desmond Downer, RAF (d.1942)

They will rise

Isaiah 40:31

Jonathan Dove

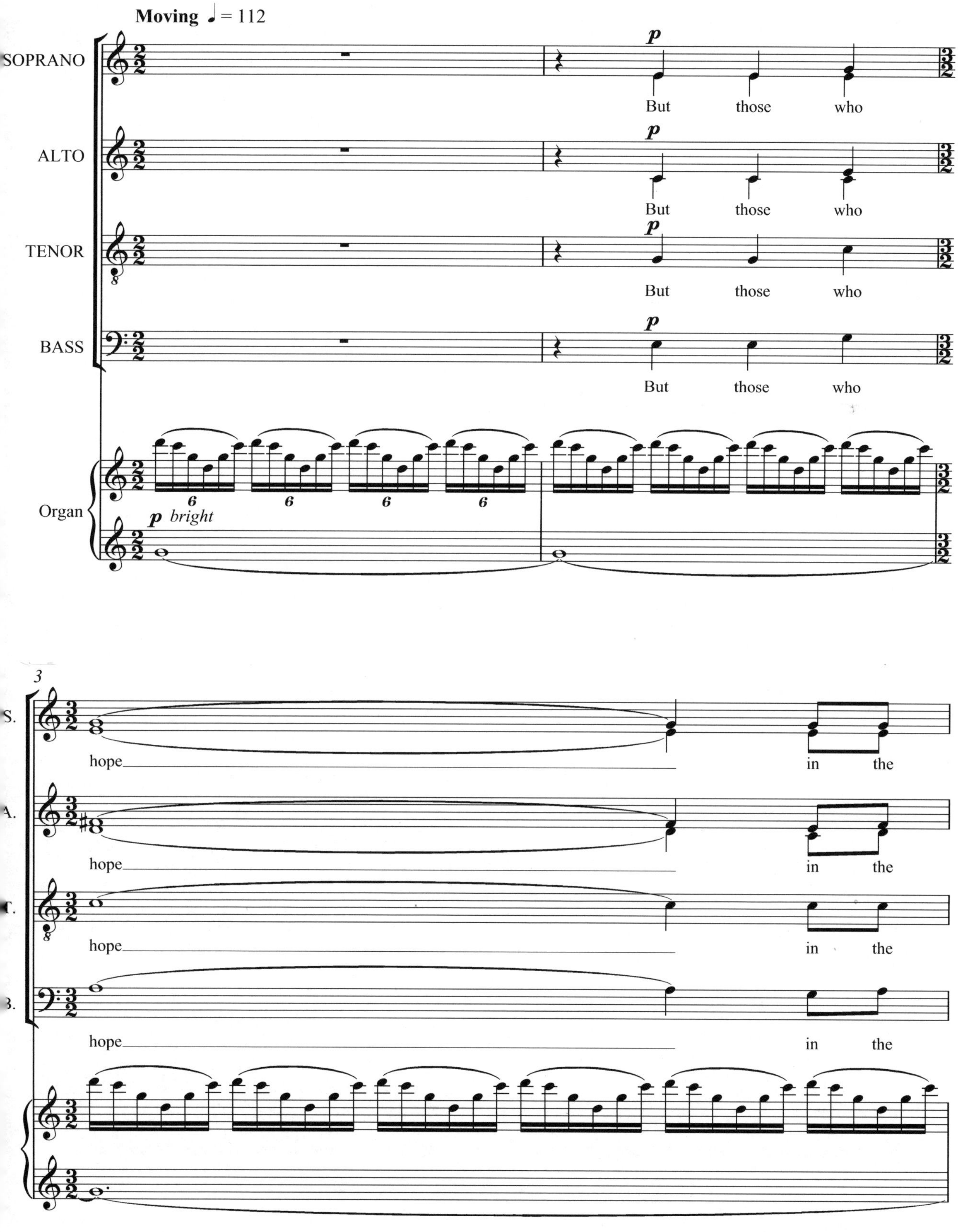

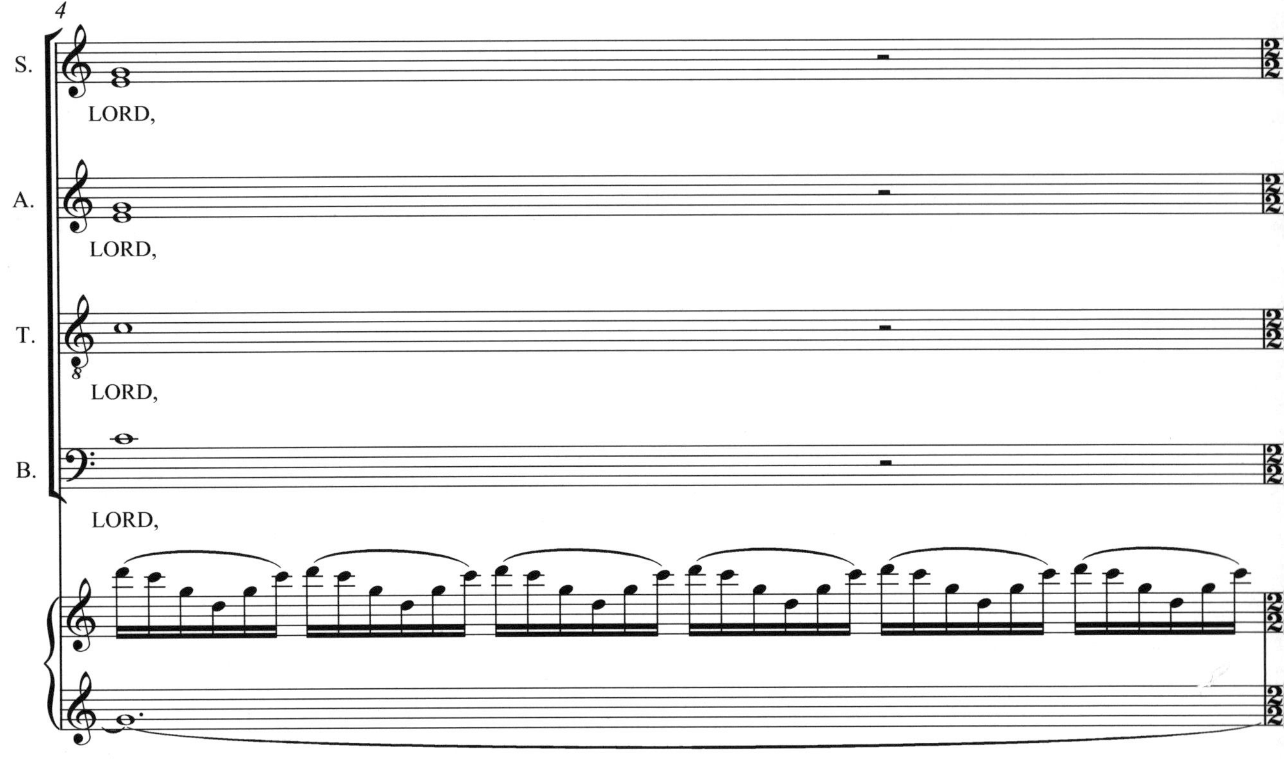
4
S.
LORD,
A.
LORD,
T.
LORD,
B.
LORD,
5 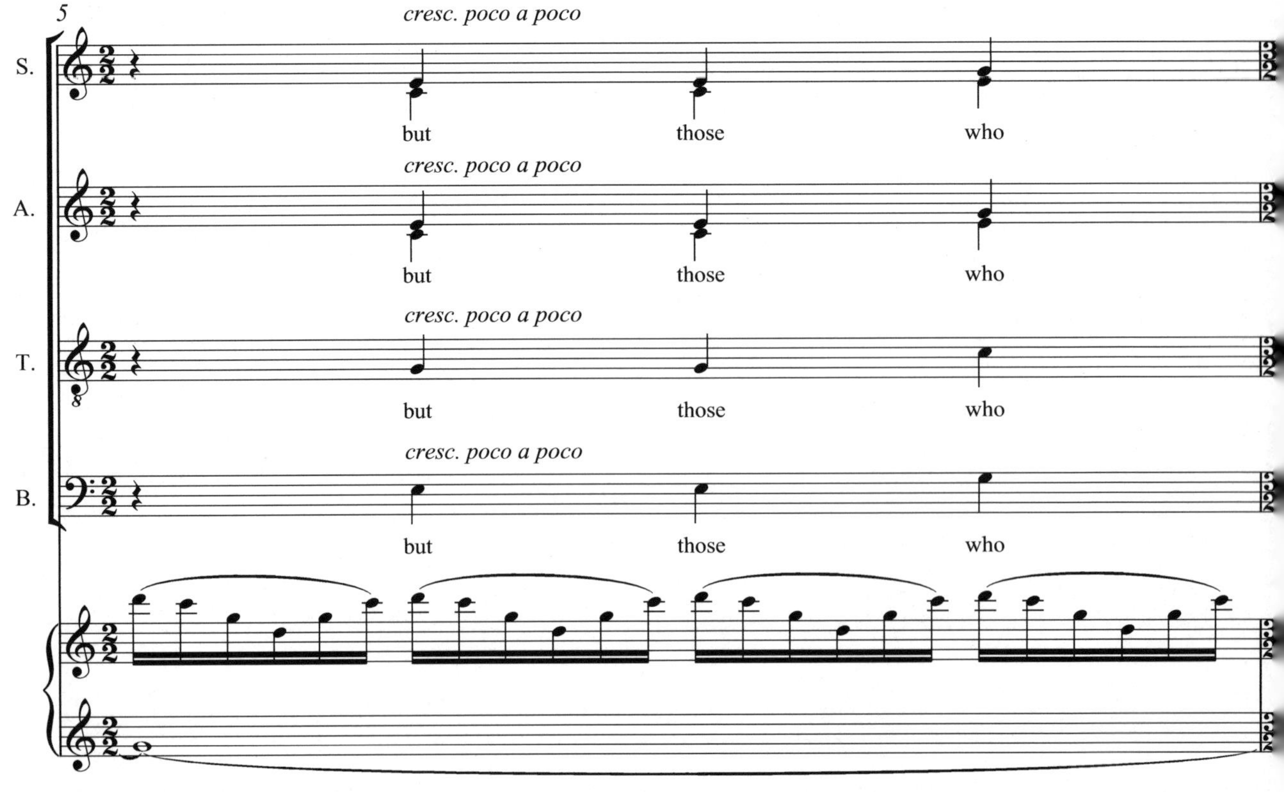
cresc. poco a poco
S.
but those who
cresc. poco a poco
A.
but those who
cresc. poco a poco
T.
but those who
cresc. poco a poco
B.
but those who

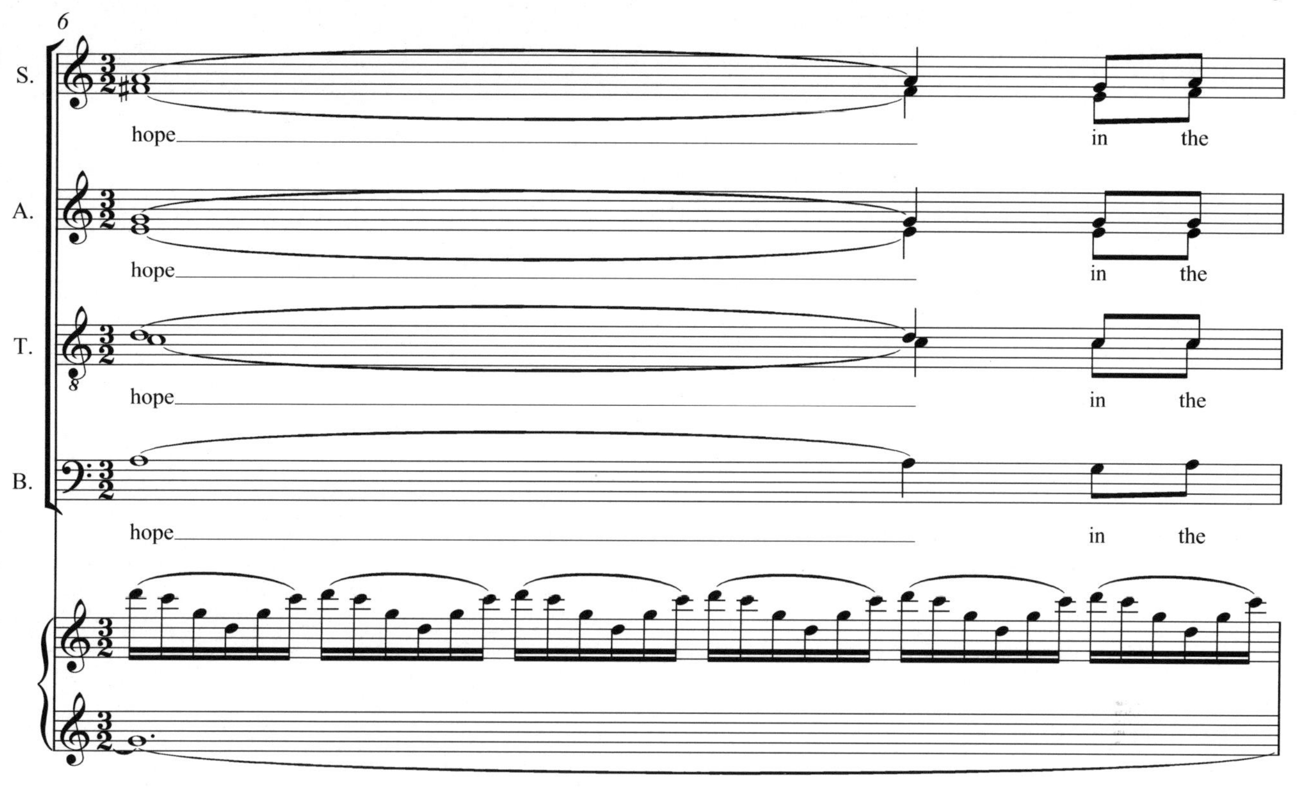

S.
A.
T.
B.
hope
hope
hope
hope
in the
in the
in the
in the

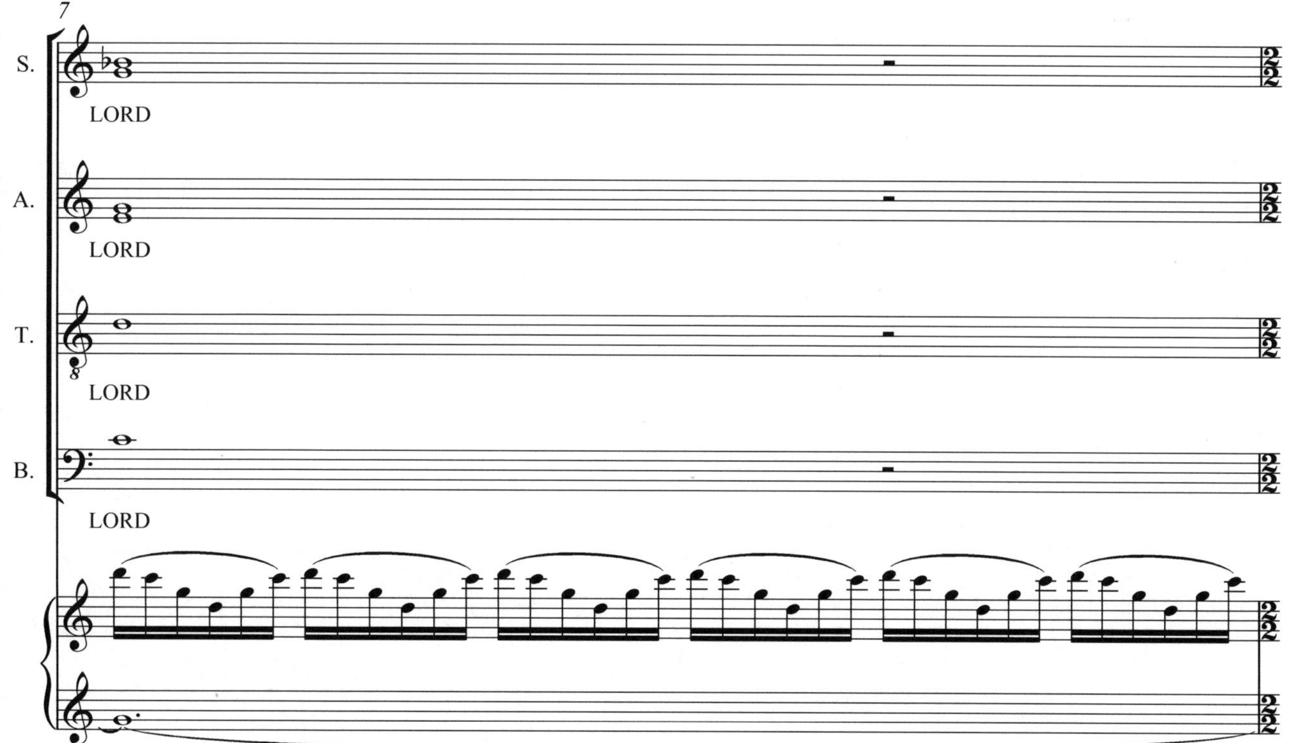

S.
A.
T.
B.
LORD
LORD
LORD
LORD

8
S.
A.
T.
B.
will re - new their
will re - new their
will re - new their
will re - new their

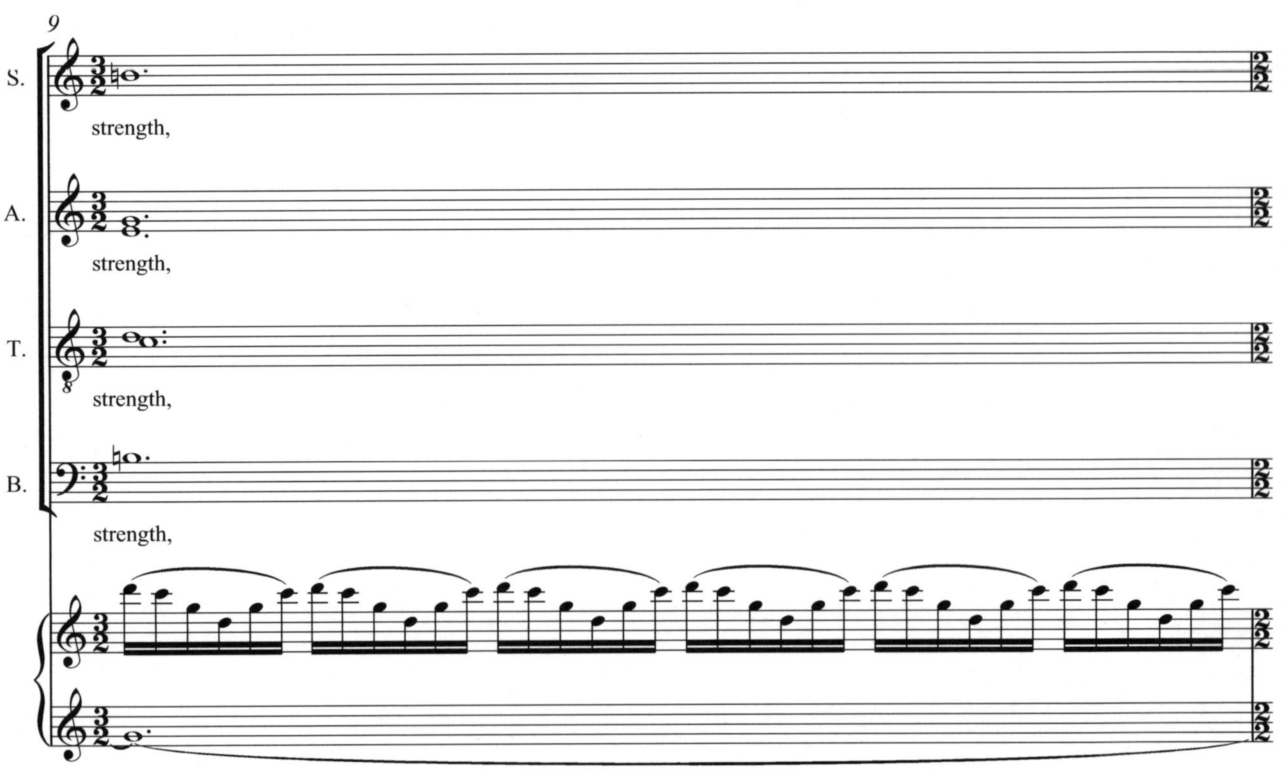
9
S.
A.
T.
B.
strength,
strength,
strength,
strength,

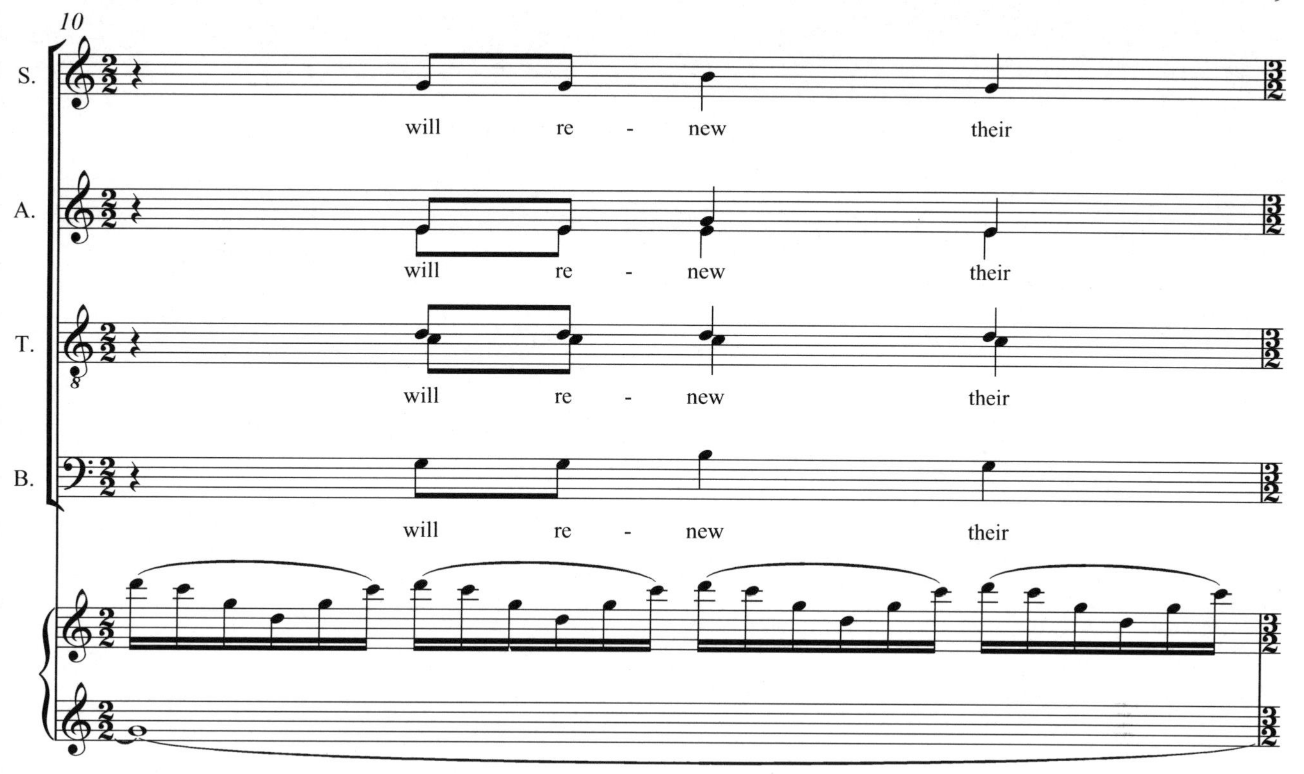

10
S.
will re - new their
A.
will re - new their
T.
will re - new their
B.
will re - new their

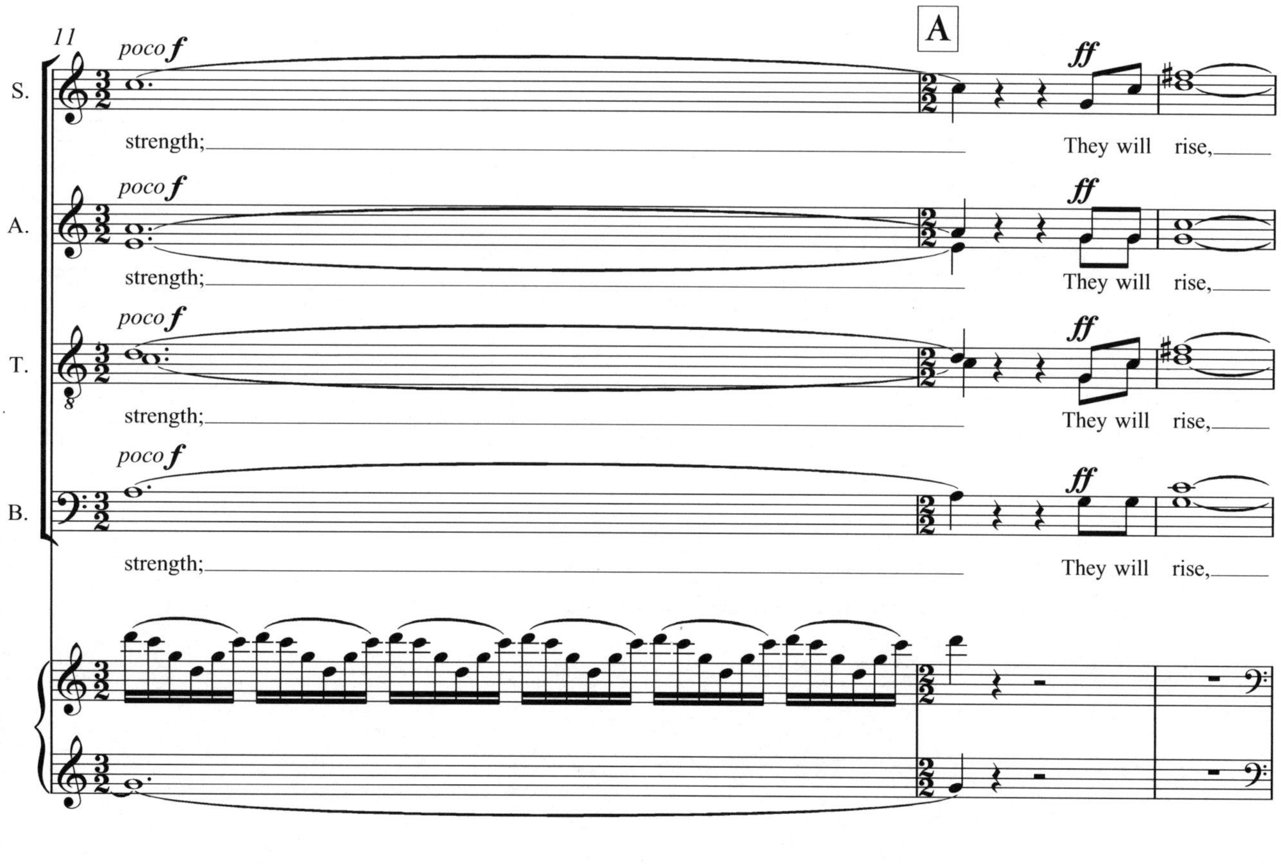
11
A
S.
poco f
strength;
ff
They will rise,
A.
poco f
strength;
ff
They will rise,
T.
poco f
strength;
ff
They will rise,
B.
poco f
strength;
ff
They will rise,

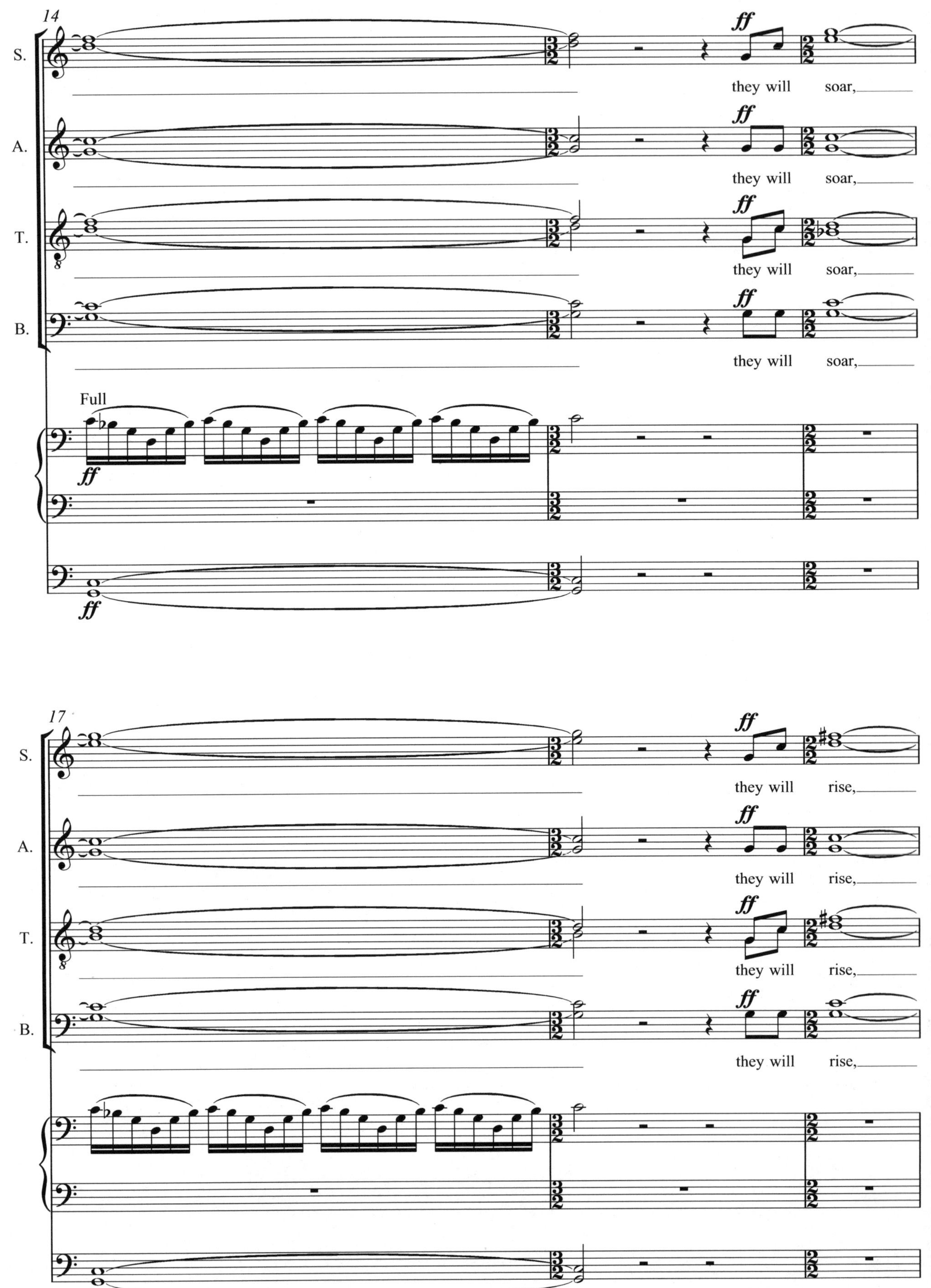
they will soar,
they will soar,
they will soar,
they will soar,
Full
they will rise,
they will rise,
they will rise,
they will rise,

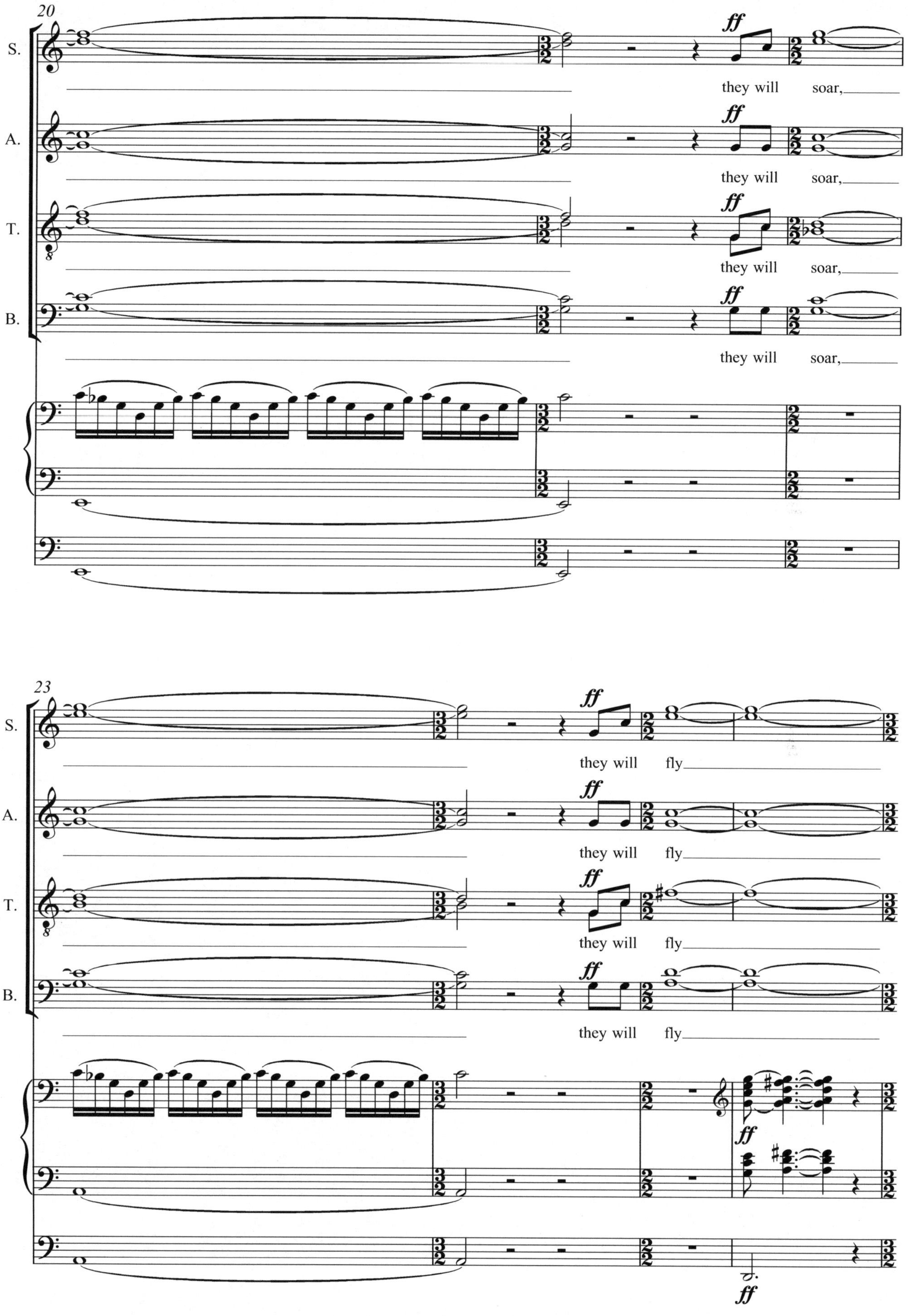
20
S.
ff
they will soar,
A.
ff
they will soar,
T.
ff
they will soar,
B.
ff
they will soar,
23
S.
ff
they will fly
A.
ff
they will fly
T.
ff
they will fly
B.
ff
they will fly
ff
ff

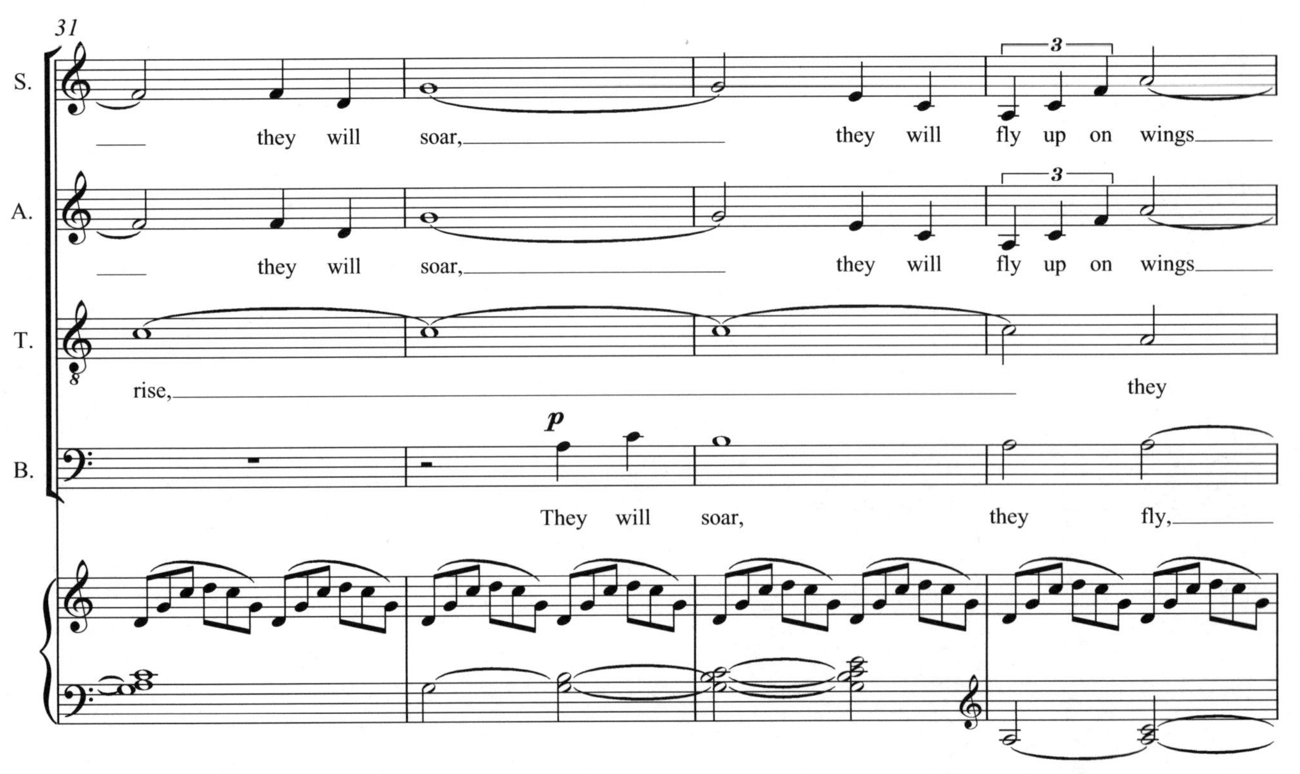
27
B
S.
A.
T.
B.
mp
mp
p
They will rise,
They will rise,
They will
Flute 8'
I
II
p
p
3
3
3
3
31
S.
A.
T.
B.
they will soar, they will fly up on wings
they will soar, they will fly up on wings
rise, they
p
They will soar, they fly,
3
3

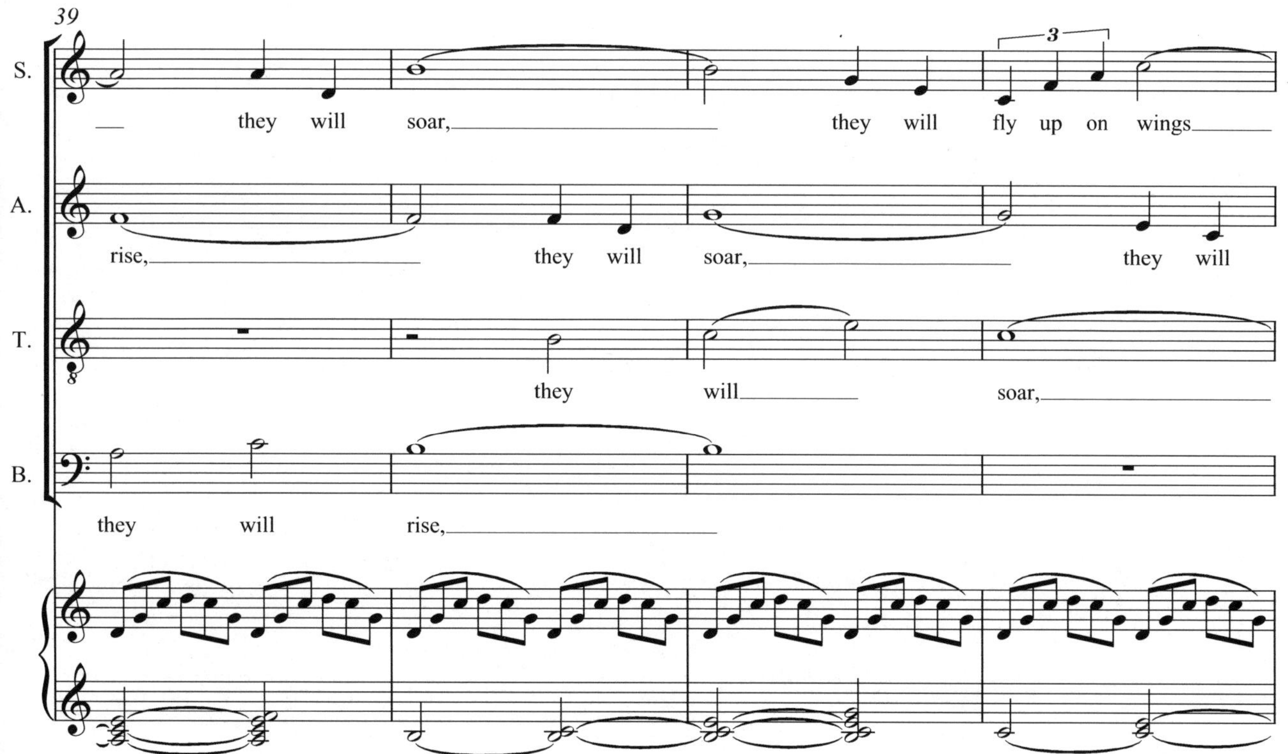
C
like ea - gles, They will rise,
like ea - gles, They will
fly, they fly,
fly,
add
they will soar, they will fly up on wings
rise, they will soar, they will
they will soar,
they will rise,

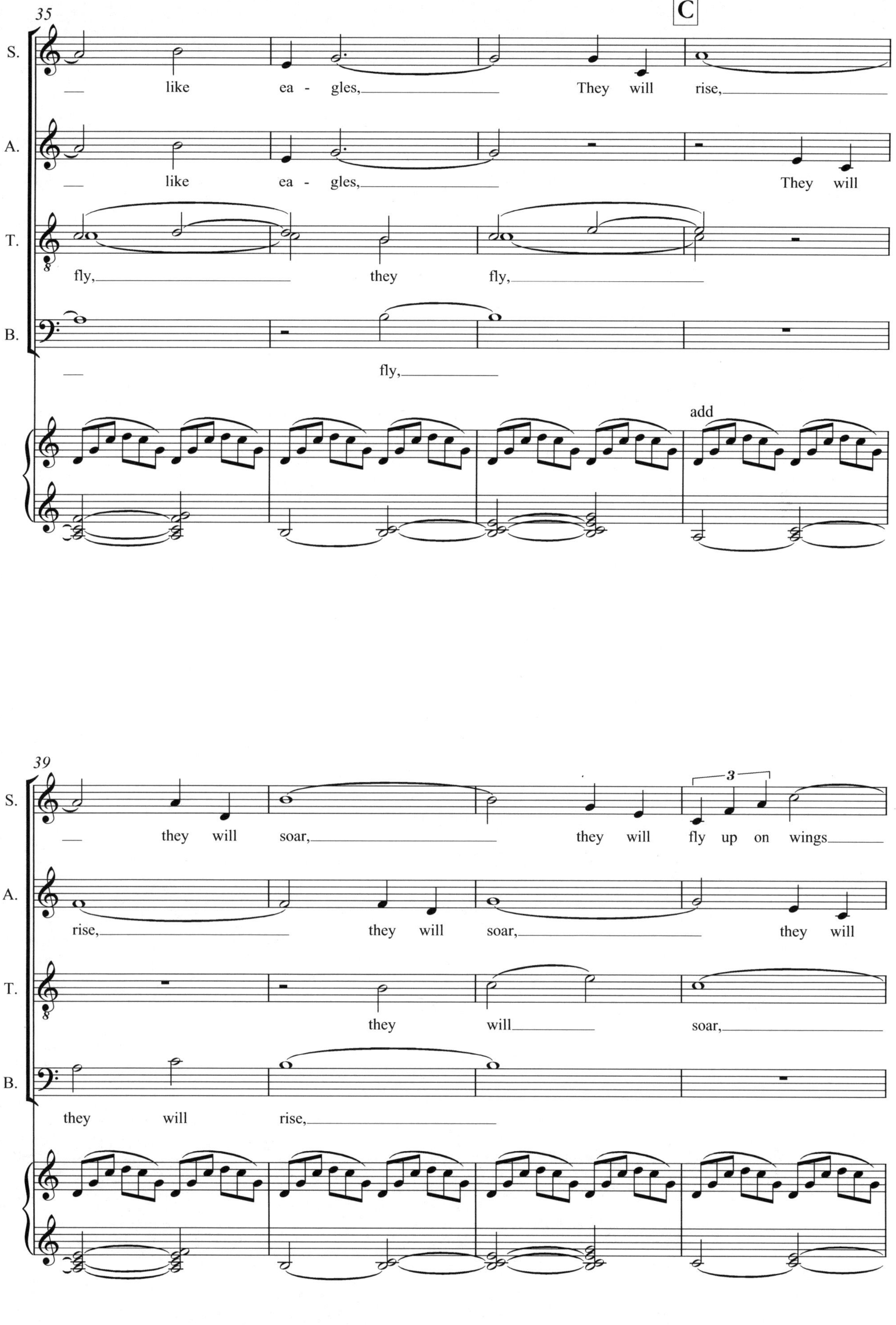

43
D
S.
A.
T.
B.
mf
mf
mp
like ea - gles, they will rise,
fly up on wings like ea - gles, they
they fly they
Mixture
mp
mp
47
S.
A.
T.
B.
they will soar, they will rise,
soar, they
fly, they fly,
They will rise,
fly, they
mp
mp

E

51
S. they will soar,_____ they will fly up on wings_____
A. soar,_____ they will fly, fly up on
T. They will fly,
B. they will fly,_____
will_____ soar,_____

55
S. like ea - gles,_____ they will fly up on wings
A. wings like ea - gles,_____ they will fly, fly up on
T. fly up on wings_____ like ea - gles, fly,
B. they will fly up on wings, ea - gles, fly,_____
they will fly up on wings, ea - gles, fly,_____

59
S.
A.
T.
B.
like ea - gles, they will fly
wings like ea - gles, they will fly, they will
fly up on wings like ea - gles,
they will fly up on wings, ea - gles, fly,
63
S.
A.
T.
B.
up on wings like
fly up on wings like
they will fly on
they will fly on

F
66
S.
ea - gles;
A.
ea - gles;
T.
wings like ea - gles;
B.
wings;
bright
mf
Trumpet
mf
69
T.
mf
They will run and not grow
72
T.
wea - ry; March on and not feel
mf
B.
March on and not feel

76
T.
B.
faint, They will run and not grow
faint, They will run and not grow
80
T.
B.
wea - ry; March on and not feel
wea - ry; March on and not feel
84
T.
B.
faint, and not feel faint.
faint, and not feel faint.

88
+ open Diapason
89
90
92 G
f
They will
A.
f
They will
Full
f
f
S.
T.
B.

16
93
S.
rise,
they will
A.
f
They
will
T.
rise,
they will
B.
f
They
will
94 
S.
soar,
they will
A.
rise,
they will
T.
soar,
they will
B.
rise,
they will

17
95
S. fly up on wings like
A. fly like
T. fly up on wings like
B. fly like
96
S. ea - gles, they will
A. ea - gles,
T. ea - gles, they will
B. ea - gles,

97 H
S. rise, they will
A. they will
T. rise, they will
B. they will
98
S. soar, they will
A. rise, they will
T. soar, they will
B. rise, they will

99
S.
A.
T.
B.
fly up on wings like
fly like
fly up on wings like
fly like
100
S.
A.
T.
B.
ea - gles, they will
ea - gles,
ea - gles, they will
ea - gles,

20
101 I
S.
A.
T.
B.
rise,
they
will
they
will
rise,
they
will
they
will
102
S.
A.
T.
B.
soar,
they
will
fly
up,
soar,
they
will
fly
up,

103
S.
A.
T.
B.
rise,
they will
they
will
rise,
they will
they
will
104
S.
A.
T.
B.
soar,
they will
soar,
they
soar,
they will
soar,
they

22
J
105 
S. fly up on wings like
A. fly up on
T. fly up on wings like
B. fly up on
106
S. ea - gles, they will
A. wings, they
T. ea - gles, they will
B. wings, they

107
S.
A.
T.
B.
fly up on wings like
fly up on
fly up on wings like
fly up on
108
S.
A.
T.
B.
ea - gles, they will
wings, they
ea - gles, they will
wings, they

109
S. fly up on
A. fly,
T. fly up on
B. fly, fly
110
S. wings like
A. fly up like
T. wings like
B. up like

111
S.
A.
T.
B.
ea - gles.
ea - gles.
ea - gles.
ea - gles.
112
S.
A.
T.
B.
They will rise.
They will rise.
They will rise.
They will rise.
ff
ff
ff
ff
ff
6
6

Jonathan Dove

Jonathan Dove (b. 1959) studied composition with Robin Holloway at Cambridge and worked as a freelance repetiteur, animateur and arranger. His first major projects came via Glyndebourne, including his breakthrough commission, the opera *Flight*, for Glyndebourne Touring Opera. Other operatic works include *The Adventures of Pinocchio*, *Swanhunter*, children's opera *The Hackney Chronicles*, *When She Died* – examining the response to the death of Diana, Princess of Wales – and *Man on the Moon*. Works for orchestra include the trombone concerto *Stargazer*, and *Moonlight Revels* for trumpet and saxophone. Dove was presented with the Ivor Novello Award for Classical Music in 2008, and in 2010 *A Song of Joys* opened the Last Night of the Proms.

Jonathan Dove (*1959) studierte bei Robin Holloway an der Universität Cambridge Komposition und arbeitete als freischaffender Korrepetitor und Arrangeur. Erste größere Werke entstanden in Zusammenarbeit mit dem englischen Glyndebourne Festival, darunter die Oper *Flight* – ein Auftragswerk der Glyndebourne Touring Opera, das ihm zum Durchbruch verhalf. Sein Opernschaffen umfasst außerdem *The Adventures of Pinocchio*, *Swanhunter*, die Kinderoper *The Hackney Chronicles*, *When She Died* – das die Reaktionen auf den Tod von Prinzessin Diana beleuchtet – sowie *Man on the Moon*. Zu seinen Orchesterwerken zählen das Posaunenkonzert *Stargazer* sowie *Moonlight Revels* für Trompete und Saxofon. 2008 erhielt Dove den Ivor Novello Award für klassische Musik, und 2010 bildete *A Song of Joys* den Auftakt zur „Last Night of the Proms".

ISMN 979-0-57701-618-4

EDITION PETERS GROUP
LEIPZIG · LONDON · NEW YORK
www.editionpeters.com

DOVE

They will rise

for SATB Choir and Organ

EDITION PETERS

EP 73257